The Nature Kid's Guide to
RATTLESNAKES

DAVID ANDERSON

For information address LP Media Inc. Publishing,
30012 Variolite St NW, Princeton MN 55371
www.lpmedia.org

Publication Data

Rattlesnakes
The Nature Kid's Guide to Rattlesnakes — First edition.

Summary: "Learn all about Rattlesnakes, the Nature Kid Way"
— Provided by publisher.

ISBN: 979-8-89818-142-0

[1. Rattlesnakes – Non-Fiction] I. Title.

Title: The Nature Kid's Guide to Rattlesnakes

CONTENTS

ROCKY RETREATS
DID YOU KNOW?
Some rattlesnakes share winter dens — hundreds of snakes pile together in the same rocky cave to stay warm!
4

**Rattle! A snake coils under a rock.
Its tail shakes a warning.**

That dry, buzzing rattle stops you cold. You freeze. You look around slowly. Somewhere nearby, a rattlesnake is patiently waiting.

Rattlesnakes are remarkable survivors. They can sense heat from a mouse hiding in the dark. They carry venom powerful enough to bring down prey much bigger than themselves. And that famous rattle on their tail has kept animals and people at a safe distance for millions of years.

There are more than thirty kinds, living everywhere from scorching deserts to cool mountain forests across North and South America.

RATTLE RANGE

Hiss! A snake slides on dry sand. It looks for shade. The sun is too hot.

Rattlesnakes live only in North and South America. Their range extends from Canada all the way to Argentina. Most make their home in the United States and Mexico, where the climate suits them best. But each species has carved out its own corner of the world.

The western diamondback rules the hot desert Southwest. Timber rattlesnakes blend into eastern forests. The ridge-nosed rattlesnake climbs high into mountain meadows. The eastern diamondback, the biggest of them all, prowls coastal lowlands near sea level.

SIZE UP

FUN
FACT!
A rattlesnake's rattle grows a new segment each time it sheds its skin!

Thump! A huge rattlesnake slithers past a log. It stretches out long.

Rattlesnakes come in a wide range of sizes. Most measure 3 to 4 feet long. But the eastern diamondback, the largest of all, can stretch up to 8 feet and weigh over 10 pounds.

Newborn babies are only about 10 inches long. They grow fast in their first years, adding size with every meal they catch.

Even the biggest rattlesnake starts life small enough to fit in the palm of your hand. By the time it is fully grown, it commands respect from almost every animal it meets.

SCALY SECRETS

DID YOU KNOW?

Rattlesnake scales overlap like shingles on a roof. This lets the body bend easily.

Snap! A snake sheds old skin. Fresh scales shine underneath.

Rattlesnakes have dry, scaly skin. Their scales are made of **keratin**, the same material in your fingernails!

Scales protect the snake's body and keep water inside. Belly scales are wide and flat, which helps the snake grip the ground.

Rattlesnakes shed their skin several times each year. Young snakes shed more often than adults. A new rattle segment forms after each shed. Old skin peels off in one long piece.

HEAT SEEKERS

FUN FACT!

12

Click! A rattlesnake flicks its tongue. It senses warmth nearby.

Rattlesnakes have a superpower most animals lack. On each side of their face, between the eye and nostril, sits a small pit organ. These pits detect heat, not light, giving rattlesnakes a kind of invisible vision.

When a warm mouse moves through darkness, the rattlesnake feels it. The pits sense body heat from up to three feet away. The snake does not need light or sound to know something is nearby.

This is why rattlesnakes are such deadly night hunters. They can track a mouse through a pitch-dark burrow.

VENOM POWER

Swoosh! A rattlesnake strikes fast. Venom flows through its fangs.

Rattlesnakes have hollow fangs. These fangs fold back when the mouth closes, then swing forward to bite.

These fangs connect to venom glands behind the eyes. When a rattlesnake bites, muscles squeeze the glands. Venom shoots through the fangs like liquid from a syringe.

Rattlesnake venom breaks down tissue and blood. This helps the snake digest its meal.

Rattlesnakes control how much venom they use. Sometimes they bite with none!

ON THE
HUNT

Sniff! A rattlesnake flicks its tongue and picks up a scent on the breeze.

Rattlesnakes eat mice, rats, and other small animals. They also catch lizards, birds, and rabbits.

Rattlesnakes do not chew their food. They swallow prey headfirst in one big gulp. Special jaws stretch wide to fit large meals.

One meal can last a rattlesnake for weeks. A large snake may eat only 10 to 12 meals per year!

Baby rattlesnakes eat tiny lizards and frogs.

SIT AND STRIKE

A rattlesnake can strike and return to its coiled position in less than one second.

Shhh! A rattlesnake waits in the grass. It stays perfectly still.

Rattlesnakes are **ambush** hunters. They do not chase their prey. Instead, they wait for food to come to them.

A rattlesnake picks a good hiding spot near animal trails. It coils its body and stays very still. The snake can wait for hours or even days.

A rattlesnake strikes in about 70 milliseconds, which is faster than a blink! The quick bite delivers **venom**. Then the snake lets go and waits. The venom works quickly, and soon the snake can safely eat its meal.

WATCH OUT

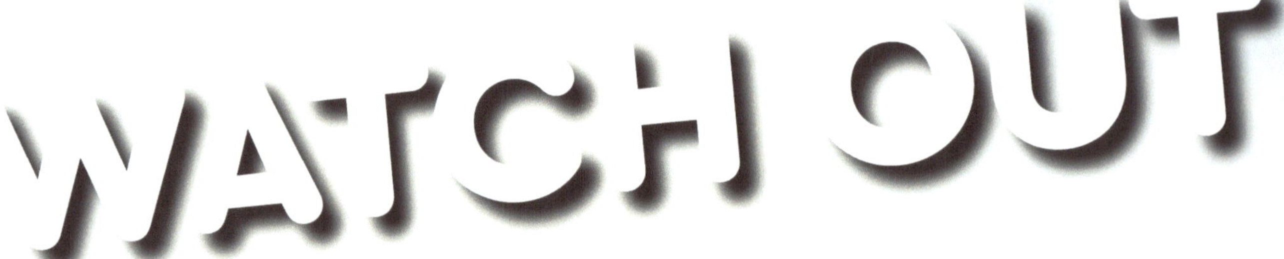

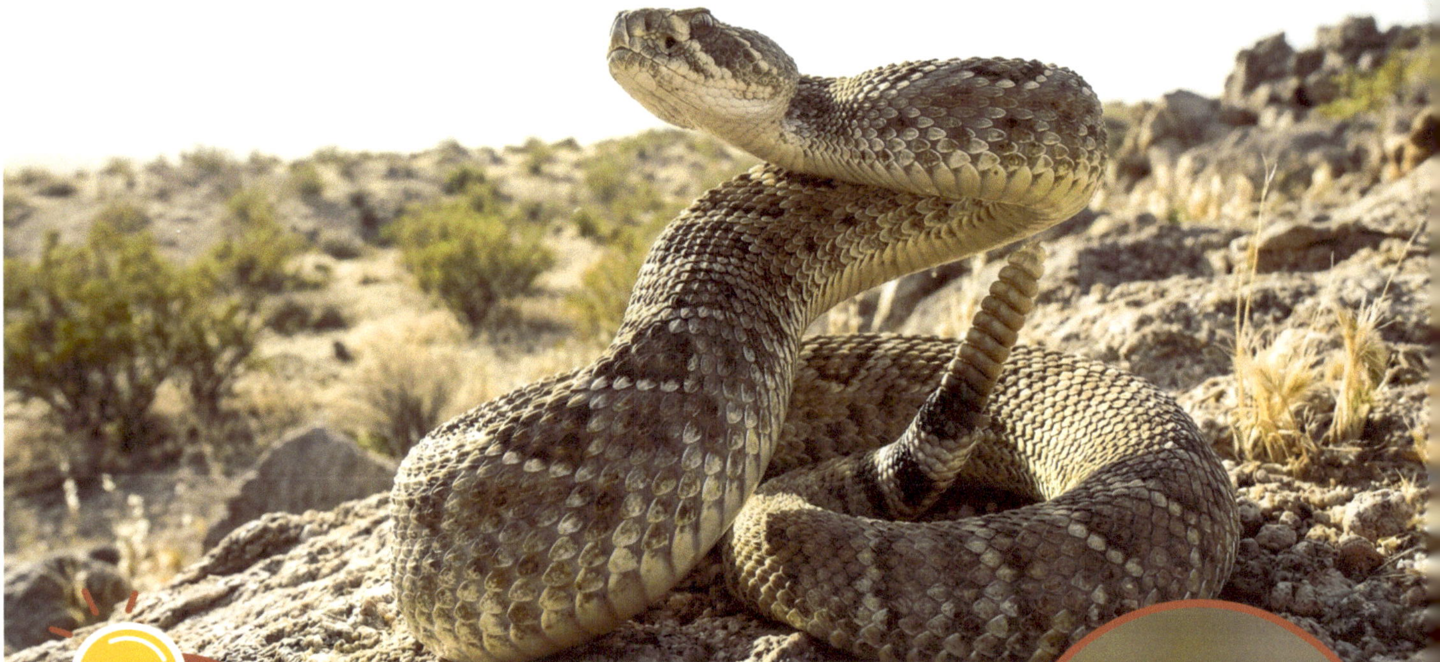

DID YOU KNOW

Roadrunners kill rattlesnakes. They peck their heads and will smash them on rocks!

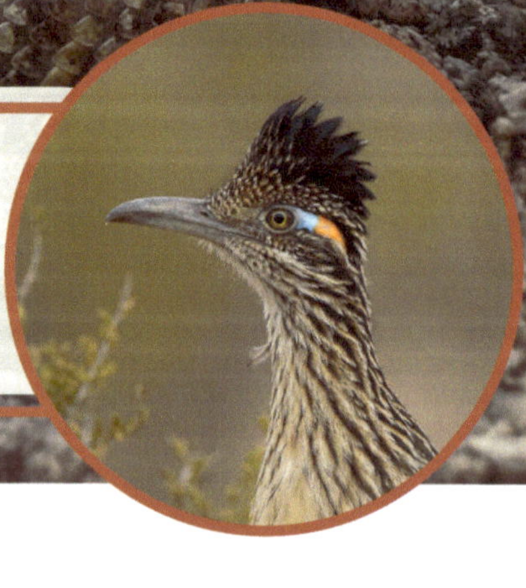

Screech! A hawk dives down. A rattlesnake coils in defense.

Rattlesnakes may be dangerous, but they have plenty of enemies of their own. Hawks, eagles, and owls hunt them from above, diving fast with sharp talons before the snake has time to react. On the ground, coyotes, foxes, and wild pigs all hunt rattlesnakes.

One of the most surprising predators is the kingsnake. Rattlesnake venom does not affect it at all. Kingsnakes simply wrap around their prey and squeeze.

Young rattlesnakes face the most danger. They are small and their rattle is barely developed, making them an easy target.

SHAKE AND HIDE

Rustle! A rattlesnake slips into a rock crack. It vanishes fast.

Rattlesnakes shake their tails to warn predators. The rattle sound says "stay away!" Most predators leave when they hear it.

If warnings fail, rattlesnakes escape. They slide into burrows, rock cracks, or thick brush. Their colors help them hide.

Hiding saves energy and keeps them safe. Fighting uses venom they need for hunting.

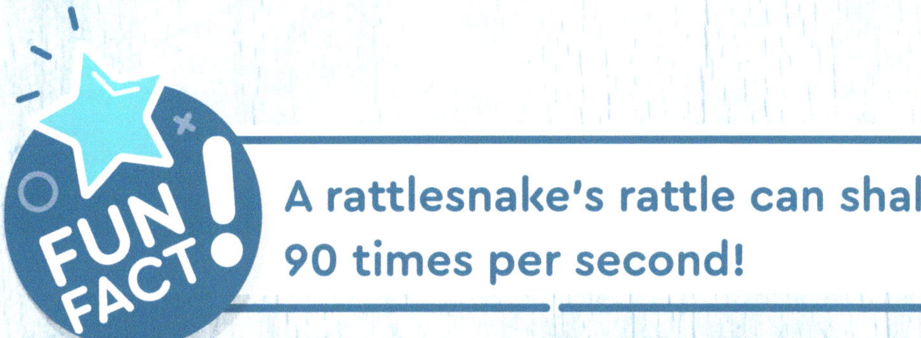

24

Whoosh! A rattlesnake glides over hot sand. Its body makes S-shaped curves.

Rattlesnakes move by bending their bodies into curves. They push against rocks and sand to slide forward.

Some rattlesnakes use sidewinding. They lift parts of their body and move sideways across loose sand. This keeps them cool.

Rattlesnakes can climb rocks and bushes. They grip with their belly scales.

Rattlesnakes have up to 200 belly scales. Each one grips the ground like a tiny shoe!

25

SUN SOAKERS

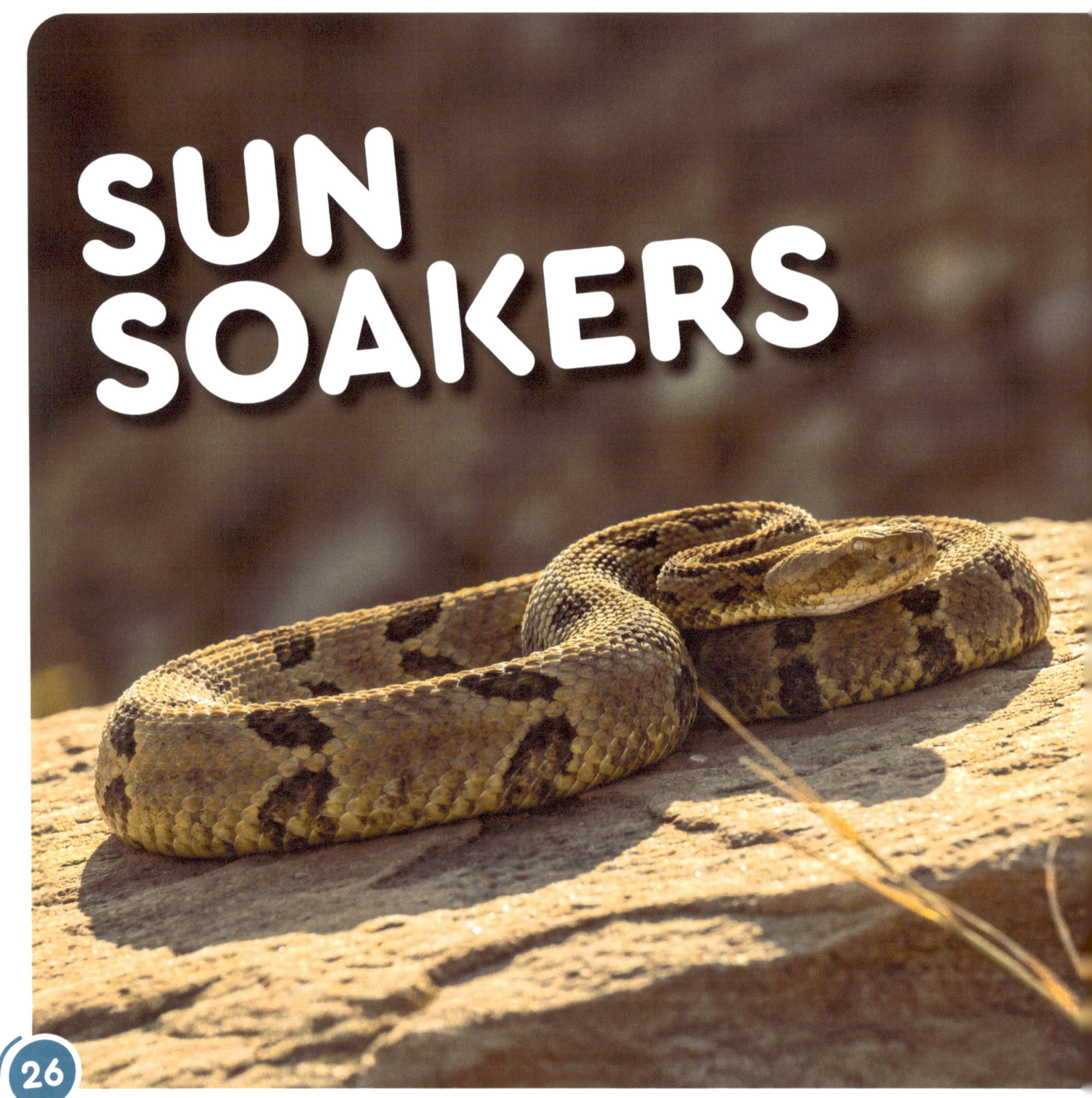

Crack! A rattlesnake stretches on a warm rock. It soaks up the sun.

Rattlesnakes are **cold-blooded**. They cannot make their own body heat, so they need the sun to warm up.

Mornings start slow for rattlesnakes. They bask on rocks or open ground, letting the sun heat their muscles.

Once warm, snakes move faster and digest food better. On hot days, they rest in shade. They move between sun and shade all day.

A rattlesnake's body temperature can change by 30 degrees in just a few hours!

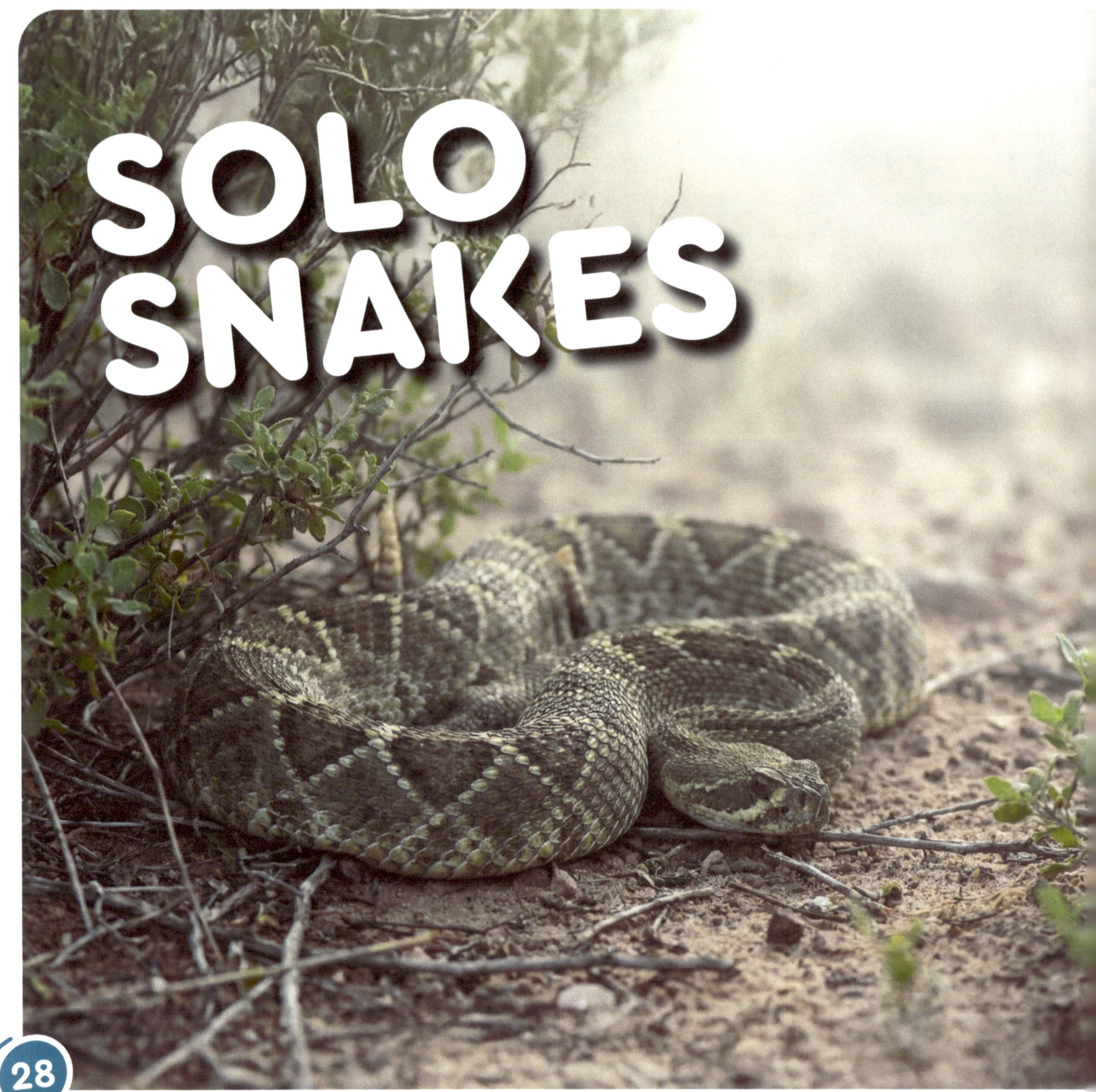

SOLO
SNAKES
28

Sssss! A rattlesnake rests under a bush. No other snakes are near.

Rattlesnakes live alone most of the time. They do not travel in groups. They do not hunt together.

Each snake finds its own food. Each snake finds its own shelter. They do not share meals. They do not help each other.

In winter, many rattlesnakes gather in dens. They pile together to stay warm. But in spring, they all go their own ways.

Rattlesnakes can recognize their own relatives by smell and will avoid harming them!

DANCE BATTLES

Stomp! Two male rattlesnakes rise up tall. They push and shove each other.

Male rattlesnakes sometimes wrestle each other. They do not bite during these fights. Instead, they push and twist with their bodies.

Each snake tries to pin the other down. They wrap around each other until one gives up. The stronger snake wins, and the loser crawls away.

These contests can last for an hour. Females often watch nearby, but they do not join in.

Male rattlesnakes can rise up to half their body length during combat dances. They never use venom.

TINY RATTLERS

Squeak! Newborn baby rattlesnakes explore outside their den.

Baby rattlesnakes are born ready to live on their own. They hatch from eggs inside their mother. So she gives birth to live babies.

Newborns are only about 10 inches long. But they already have fangs and venom. Baby rattlesnakes do not hunt right away. They wait one to two weeks.

Young snakes have a small button on their tail. This button does not rattle yet. Each time they shed skin, a new part grows. After a few sheds, they can make noise.

GO SOLO

DID YOU KNOW?
Baby rattlesnakes have a small button, not a rattle, at birth!

Snarl! A mother snake slithers away. Her babies are on their own.

Mother rattlesnakes stay with their babies for one to two weeks. She keeps watch but does not teach them anything. She does not need to.

Baby rattlesnakes are born already knowing how to hunt, sense heat, and inject venom. Every skill they need to survive comes built in from the moment they enter the world. No other training required.

Newborn rattlesnakes are actually more dangerous than adults in one way. Young snakes have not yet learned to control how much venom they inject, so their bites can deliver a full dose every time.

TOUGH SURVIVORS

Crunch! A rattlesnake crawls through dry fall leaves.

Rattlesnakes are built to survive. While other animals struggle through harsh conditions, rattlesnakes simply slow down and wait them out.

When winter arrives, they sink into a deep sleep called **hibernation**, tucked into rocky dens sometimes shared with hundreds of other snakes. Their heart rate drops, their body nearly stops, and they can go months without a single meal.

When spring finally warms the rocks above, they wake up exactly where they left off — ready to go again.

STAY SAFE

Most rattlesnake bites happen when people try to touch, catch, or kill the snake.

Rattle! A hiker spots a snake on the trail. She backs away slowly.

Rattlesnakes almost never want trouble with people. That rattle is a warning, not a threat. The snake is saying back off, and the smart move is to listen.

If you hear a rattle, freeze immediately. Do not jump or run. Look around slowly, find the snake with your eyes, then back away calmly and give it plenty of room to move on.

When hiking in rattlesnake country, wear boots and long pants. Never reach under rocks, logs, or into brush where you cannot see, and watch every step on rocky trails.

GLOSSARY

keratin

A hard material that makes up snake scales.

venom

A poison that snakes make to help them catch and eat their food.

ambush

A way of hunting by hiding and waiting for food to come close.

cold-blooded

An animal that needs the sun to warm up its body.

hibernation

To sleep through the cold winter months in a safe hiding spot.